GW00586514

# Poems
# Of
# The
# Cities

## Professor M. R. Ali

## Multimedia Publishing

**Poems Of The Cities**

**Published by**

Multimedia Publishing

Artology International

The Chalet House, Golf Club Road,
St. George's Hill, Weybridge,
Surrey, KT13 0NN, England.

British Library cataloguing in publication data.
A catalogue record for this book is available from the British Library.

Printed in Hong Kong

ISBN 1 899873 00 7

# CONTENTS

To poetry lovers
and city dwellers
everywhere.

# INTRODUCTION

For centuries every significant Arabic poet, from Al-Mutanabi to Al-Jawahri, was born in a special region south of Baghdad. The shape and the geographical location of this special region is a unique poetic basin extending along the rich and fertile lands of the Euphrates and Tigris, and the hostile desert stretching to Jordan, in the west, and deep in the Arabian Peninsula, in the south. With such an environment the famous Arabic poetry nourished. This unique poetic basin became the poetsland.

I was born in the poetsland, and more precisely in the lovely town of Karbela where every other kid dreamed of becoming a poet, like nowadays in the West every other kid dreams of becoming a film star. We all knew that not everybody could make a living from writing, reading or reciting poems, but nevertheless all kids took the subject of poetry very seriously, whether inside or outside school. On average, every kid learned hundreds of verses and was able to take part in poetic competitions, in the hope of one day achieving the coveted poetdom.

Gradually the dreams of most kids shifted to the hard facts of reality and, as youths, we started placing ourselves in suitable positions to make realistic careers, far away from the poetic fantasy. Scientific and engineering subjects replaced literature and poetry in secondary schools. The trend in my childhood was to avoid all types of arts and all types of sports, and to concentrate instead on mathematical and scientific subjects which put you ahead of others in achieving the right education. Like other youths I dropped literature, poetry, arts and sport to be an engineer.

In ten years of education, my life was transformed from a youth born south of Baghdad to a Professor of Technology attending international acoustic congresses all over the world. Indeed, engineering helped me to make a lucrative and profitable career, but I had not given up my poetic roots. For twenty years I was living in exile from any poetic input; I neither heard nor read any poems, either in Arabic or English.

The reader may wonder how I ended up writing poems in English and about cities. The answer is that, when I visited New York to promote Deltaism, an artform I generated, my agent was more impressed with my poetry than with my paintings. My first poem of a city started in New York when I described it as a City of Hunger. From that time I was able to paint cities with words. The descriptive poems of London, Tokyo, Paris, Madrid, Dublin, Helsinki, Rome, Cairo, Jerusalem and Moscow attracted the attention of my friends, and when I received letters of thanks from Chancellor Helmut Kohl of Germany and the Mayor of Berlin for the poem of Berlin, I realised that poems of the cities have a wide appeal.

My recital of Stockholm, a Darling City, and the applause of the crowd of international art critics in the famous Town Hall–in the presence of the Mayor–in October 1994, made me feel and believe that poetry is, as it was, appreciated by a wide range of people. Such belief and feeling are the factors behind my sharing my experience in the poetic voyage of the cites with friends and readers. To enrich this collection of the poems of the cities, I added Beijing, a City of Wisdom, Delhi, a City of Legend, Pretoria, a City of a New Start, and Sydney, the Harbour. I also included an Ideal City a phantasmal concept. For the time being, let us read and recite the poems of the cities and enjoy the pleasure they can offer.

In conclusion, The descriptive poems of the cities that are in your hands are an attempt to paint true and real pictures in words of cities that we admire and respect.

# POEM FOR BERLIN

*Be in Berlin when history is written,*
*Be in Berlin when events happen,*
> *Be in Berlin, Berlin, Berlin.*

*East Berlin where emotions span,*
*West Berlin where response began,*
> *Be in Berlin, Berlin, Berlin.*

*Over the wall where fears started,*
*Over the wall where lovers parted,*
> *Be in Berlin, Berlin, Berlin.*

*Be in Berlin when freedom calls,*
*Be in Berlin when the wall falls,*
> *Be in Berlin, Berlin, Berlin.*

*See in Berlin the happy faces,*
*See in Berlin the joy of all races,*
> *Be in Berlin, Berlin, Berlin.*

*Be in Berlin – Europe's youngest bride,*
*Be in Berlin – German's latest pride,*
> *Be in Berlin, Berlin, Berlin.*

## NO OTHER CITY

*No other city*

*Like this city*

*Enriched humanity*

*As Cairo the eternity*

*The city of immortality*

## *DELHI THE LEGEND*

*From Piccadilly to Delhi,*
*Make the pilgrimage yearly,*
*Over the oceans over the seas,*
*To the land of mysteries.*
        *Delhi is a legend.*

*The sound of mystery*
*Sung throughout history,*
*Heard by every generation,*
*Practised on every occasion.*
        *Delhi is a legend.*

*Dressing the traditional dress,*
*Glittering like a princess,*
*Celebrating your pageantry,*
*Riding high in pleasantry.*
        *Delhi is a legend.*

*Attracting kings, emperors,*
*Maharajas and conquerors,*
*To build world wonders,*
*And to introduce new flavours.*
        *Delhi is a legend.*

*In a class of its own,*
*A new civilization was born,*
*Radiating knowledge and harmony,*
*Plenty of wealth and money.*
      *Delhi is a legend.*

*Looking for a new role,*
*Setting high its goal,*
*Playing the power of persuasion,*
*As a weapon for determination.*
      *Delhi is a legend.*

*Time after time it discovered,*
*A new lead had to be offered*
*To satisfy the masses,*
*Regardless of their classes.*
      *Delhi is a legend.*

*It took the bold initiative,*
*Asking a dear son to be active,*
*To deliver peaceful appeals,*
*A new wave of human ideals.*
      *Delhi is a legend.*

*The son obeyed the order,*
*And contained the disorder.*
*With his blood had written,*
*Peaceful coexistence is unbeaten.*
            *Delhi is a legend.*

*The legendary city*
*Has a new identity.*
*A city of peace, tranquillity,*
*Democracy and diversity.*
            *Delhi is a legend.*

*Dignitaries and visitors witness,*
*The air of richness,*
*Blowing through exotic spices,*
*And through sceneries from*
*paradises.*
            *Delhi is a legend.*

*From Delhi to Piccadilly,*
*We made the pilgrimage surely,*
*Back to the land of inspiration,*
*From the land of meditation.*

## *THE MOTHER CITY*

*From her Celtic origin,*
*Her name is given.*
*To her the Irish listen,*
*As Mother Dublin.*


*Dublin is a caring Irish mother,*
*Loving her sons and daughters,*
*Who are scattered the world over.*
*She recalls and remembers.*


*Celebrating St Patrick's Day,*
*When her children pray,*
*At the Cathedral bay,*
*And what do they say?*


*You are the mother of all mothers,*
*Your children and grandchildren,*
*To you will always listen.*
*You are the great Mother Dublin.*

## RAINBOW SMILE CITY

*Wrapped in white –*
*The bell is ringing;*
*A bridal city*
*Ready for its wedding.*


*Your winter marriage*
*To your nature*
*Is a remarkable scene*
*For a beautiful picture!*


*The snow is falling*
*Away from it all.*
*Somewhere in the North*
*Thinking of your goal.*


*With a hot sauna*
*On a frozen lake –*
*Then cups of coffee*
*And a piece of cake.*

*Now the time is right,*
*For a long restful night;*
*With beautiful nature*
*Holding you tight.*

*Dreaming of what will be –*
*A year of fantasy?*
*Four seasons to enter*
*Now the Winter is over.*

*The long dark nights*
*Have gone away;*
*Say hello to the Spring –*
*And its May Day.*

*Now you emerge*
*As a fair green bride –*
*Fresh, from your long*
*Winter's hide.*

*As a city of colours*
*Attracting each others*
*With the forest and its wonders*
*As a stage for the lovers.*


*Your Spring is delightful*
*There are good times ahead*
*For dippers in your fountains*
*Or serenaders of your mermaid.*


*Now is the time for Summer*
*When everyone gathers*
*Right in the centre,*
*parading with each other.*


*As if the time is right*
*For a drink or a fight!*
*Or a friendly chat,*
*Of what is this and what is that.*

*Helsinki is the place to be,*
*To be seen and to see,*
*To agree and to disagree –*
*Of whatever may be.*

*Midsummer night is a forum*
*For the hopeful.*
*A memorable time –*
*If you are watchful.*

*The fire of eternity*
*Warms your hopes and memory –*
*Till next Summer,*
*As a time to remember.*

*Soon the forest will be crying*
*For birds are migrating,*
*The weather is changing,*
*And Autumn is coming.*

*The leaves are changing colours*
*Signalling the time is over.*
*A new season enters –*
*And now the wild for wilders.*

*The dark is spreading,*
*Candlelights are glowing*
*Your independence celebration*
*Is the next occasion.*

*Relax, count your blessings –*
*And remember*
*The happenings*
*Since last Winter.*

*A city has earned a lot*
*In names, events and what is not*
*A rainbow-smile city*
*Is part of your identity.*

*But you are known*
*As Daughter of the Baltic.*
*And to all your friends,*
*You will always be magic.*

*But to me*
*You remain*
*The inspiring place*
*With a beautiful face.*

## JERUSALEM *(CITY OF HOPE)*

*The city of hope*

*That shines at the top*

*With the torch of forgiveness*

*For peace and progress*

## THE TRAVELLING CITY

London is a travelling city,
That travelled throughout history,
From here to eternity,
A city of charm and mystery.


Although on the Thames,
Is your location,
The Seven Seas
Were your destination.


Ruling the waves,
Of all kinds,
And never been slave,
In body or mind.


Flying high in the sky,
Watching and watched,
To whom and by whom,
You are the torch.

*Have you stopped or slept,*
*Have you wondered,*
*What had happened to the rest,*
*Do you know you are the best?*


*Now tell me where*
*You have been,*
*And tell me the tales,*
*And the stories of what you've seen.*

\*\*\*


*Now that I have survived,*
*Passed the test of time,*
*Endured the unexpectable,*
*And proved insurmountable.*


*After I was born,*
*I was sworn,*
*To be a travelling city,*
*Of charm and history.*

*Living up to that challenge,*
*Being a centre of attraction,*
*Exposing myself,*
*To all intentions.*

*Then I became a teenager,*
*Caring for no one,*
*In world affairs,*
*I took it as fun.*

*With my admirers,*
*Running everywhere,*
*I showed them the way,*
*On the top, to stay.*

*In vigour and resoluteness,*
*I believed,*
*Fleets of everything,*
*Were enjoyable indeed.*

*Everyone was in a group,*
*Massing for what was to be,*
*An army of discovery,*
*For my wish and my fantasy.*

*Soon I became,*
*The city of fame,*
*To all seekers,*
*And to all revealers.*

*The fun of exploration,*
*For the sake of excitation,*
*Which was my initiation,*
*Became pure adulation.*

*I became a professional traveller,*
*At an early age,*
*Setting the world as audience,*
*And my city as stage.*

*Now I have admirers and fleets,*
*Of everything I need –*
*Staging the time for a show,*
*For everybody to follow.*


*To achieve something –*
*First something new,*
*To be honoured,*
*In the list of the few.*


*Such a trend began first,*
*To appear everywhere,*
*Spreading fast,*
*From the start to the end.*


*Then the city of imagination,*
*Was led,*
*By an adventurous team,*
*Bound for new destinations.*

*For an excess of obsession,*
*Screaming of approval or denial,*
*To the poor or the Royal,*
*To the leaver, to the arrival.*

*Now I am no longer a teen,*
*Travelled all around,*
*Have been where I have been,*
*And all races I have seen.*

*I wanted to be,*
*The new lady,*
*Leading my city,*
*To its new destiny.*

*"Now my town",*
*I declared,*
*"Is my crown,*
*In my hand".*

*Let it be what will be,*
*Now the city lady,*
*Of mystery,*
*Had entered history.*

*Everything had started,*
*To take shape in its place,*
*Building here and building there,*
*Then London had a new face.*

*Making order from disorder,*
*Giving names to all events,*
*An establishment for who is who,*
*And information of what to do.*

*From Big Ben the news span,*
*To the world,*
*A new era,*
*Had began.*

*London is talking,*
*Through its speakers,*
*In Hyde Park,*
*And other corners.*

*My speeches,*
*Never ended,*
*And my talks,*
*Were splendid.*

*I am speaking,*
*To world subjects,*
*All we need,*
*Is real objects.*


*London is calling,*
*For world listeners,*
*Not to surrender,*
*Is the freedom.*


*Just spread the news,*
*That everyone has views,*
*Of what to choose,*
*And of what to do.*


*Choosing the travelling city,*
*As the city of hopes,*
*For the coming generation,*
*On the move and never stops.*

*Now I have travelled enough,*
*And I have slept rough,*
*Seen what I have seen,*
*I have grown wise and tough.*

*Now I am back,*
*Where I belong*
*On the River Thames,*
*Where I feel strong.*

*Let it be,*
*What to be?*
*London is the place,*
*To be.*

*Let it be,*
*What to be?*
*London is the place,*
*For me.*

## *A SISTER CITY*

*Madrid is a sister city*
*Married to her history*
*A pretty young lady*
*With fortune and destiny*


*Your sisters are scattered*
*From Seville to Malaga*
*From Barcelona to Granada*
*And the beautiful Al Hambra*


*Your family of fame and power*
*Gave you all it could offer*
*A regal identity*
*As the future world city*


*Soon you became on orphan*
*Living alone on your own*
*Refusing adoption*
*Giving no reason*

*Remembering your past*
            *Which passed so fast*
*Looking to the future*
            *With fears and tears*

*Do you remember*
            *And who can answer?*
*Where is your father?*
            *And where is your mother?*

*Do you remember*
            *And who can answer?*
*Where are your sisters?*
            *And where your brothers?*

*Do you remember*
            *And who can answer?*
*Where are your sons?*
            *And where your daughters?*

*Do you remember*
            *And who can answer?*
*Where are your admirers?*
            *And where are your lovers?*

*Adopting the gypsy strange habits*
          *Of fortune telling*
*Dancing, serenading*
          *And bull fighting*

*Soon they became your features –*
          *The big sister*
*Became a world gypsy traveller*
          *Spreading her habits all over*

*From Latin America to Africa*
          *And to everywhere*
*The Spanish tongue and habits*
          *Shone with status and merits*

*The caring sister with big dreams*
          *Never ran out of steam*
*Declaring her strategy*
          *For the worldwide Spanish community*

*They will be her loyal subjects*
          *And with their oath and her faith*
*She will reach*
          *The four corners of the earth*

*Spanish Kings and Queens*
        *Worked out the future scenes*
*How to launch the Armadas*
        *In the battles of the seas*

*Like every time before*
        *The gypsy had warned*
*Of what she had seen*
        *A turbulent sea was the scene*

*The gypsy knew, and only*
        *If the sister viewed*
*The crystal ball*
        *Just before the fall*

*The fall followed*
        *By unhappy periods*
*A time of reckoning*
        *For the next happening*

*The wise people*
        *Became available*
*For friendly advice*
        *Of how to throw the future dice*

Soon became clear
        The people were divided
Before they had started
        As foes they had parted


The division lead to trouble
        Civil War became visible
No side was able
        To control the situation


The ambitious factions
        Triggered a revolution
The Civil War had started
        The sister went to hide


Wearing black and red
        Crying and weeping for the dead
Listening to what was said
        Of the future that lay ahead

*The sister had decided*
      *Disturbances to be subsided*
*Civil War had to stop*
      *Bringing truce and hope*


*She had studied all options*
      *Of her coming actions*
*She called on a general lover*
      *To give her city peace and order*


*The lover obeyed the order*
      *Contained the disorder*
*Proclaimed himself leader*
      *And deserted the sister*


*The sister became clever*
      *Hiding under cover*
*Watching all over*
      *And waiting for the future*

*People had realised*
        *The sister was right*
*In her they believed*
        *Madrid had to lead*


*A shining image*
        *For wisdom and courage*
*A Royal Madrid*
        *Mother of all needs*


*Now you are a world city*
        *With a flamenco identity*
*Entertaining as you wish*
        *From Royalty to celebrity*


*But don't forget*
        *Your roots and Spain*
*Where the rain falls*
        *Mainly in the plain!*

## *THE NAUGHTY CITY*

*Moscow is a naughty city!*
*Flirting with her history,*
*Divorcing the old,*
*And marrying the pretty.*
> *Flirting all night and day*
> *To feel happy in any way —*
> *She loves to obey and disobey*
> *Her lovers have no say.*

*Her lovers are numbered,*
*In history books have entered*
*From Catherine the Great*
*To Gorby of late!*
> *Courting Czars and Commissars*
> *Lenin and Stalin in between —*
> *And now she is keen*
> *On hippies and yuppies.*
> *OR*
> *(On a visit from the Queen)*

*During the nights*
*She starts her fantasy,*
*Dreaming of reality*
*As her ecstasy.*

*That is why her nights*
*Are the glittering nights,*
*Starting with a vodka and a bite –*
*Dancing till the morning light.*
*Moscow nights are the nights*
*After dark and after eight*
*All start for a start*
*From the heart to the heart.*

*Moscow nights are the nights*
*After dark and after eight*
*All trips to love and hate*
*And every trip has its fate.*
*Moscow nights are the nights*
*With a trip everywhere*
*With the fresh air in your ears –*
*All melodies you can hear.*

*Moscow nights are the nights*
*With a trip all around*
*With the sound of balalaika*
*With the dance of ballerina.*
*Moscow nights are the nights*
*Take a trip through the streets*
*Take a trip; see the sights*
*Take a trip for a treat.*

*Moscow nights are the nights*
*Take a chance on a stranger*
*To her heart you can enter*
*She is shy and you are eager*

*Moscow nights are the nights*
*In her charm and in her arms*
*You can whisper of an offer*
*As her lover true forever.*

*Moscow and her nights*
*Of friendly Muscovites*
*With smiles on their faces*
*Warm welcome in all places.*

*Now let us sing and dance*
*In this naughty city*
*To which we all love to go*
*To taste her hospitality.*

*Let's all see the Moscow show*
*Moscow, where we all must go.*
*Moscow is the place to go*
*In Moscow – we can all go-go!*

# CITY OF HUNGER

*The city of hunger, created wonders*
*For the world to remember*
*Its splendours*
*Forever.*

*Marking its contrasts,*
*The slow and the fast,*
*Echoing happenings*
*Of present and past.*

*Hungry people who came*
*On the pilgrimage of fame*
*Searched for dreams*
*To achieve their aims.*

*To some, the city of hunger*
*Was a dream,*
*But to others*
*A dream that never came.*

*Walking along avenues*
*Checking every move*
*In the daily play...*
*Another day added to the news.*

*The Lady of Liberty standing high*
*Guiding all to the shore*
*Of safety and dreams*
*With her torch, showing the way*

*To the people who came from far away,*
*Enchanted by the charm that shone*
*Over the oceans, for all devotions*
*Attracting a glimpse of what would be*
*The sea green queen of mystery.*

*You are the gift of the gifted to the forgotten*
*You are the symbol of courage to the scared*
*You are the hope for the deprived*
*You are the shelter for the persecuted*

*There has never been,*
*So honoured a queen,*
*To all worldly subjects,*
*Regardless of creed.*

*To whom you belong*
*A queen so strong*
*Without a court*
*Ruling no one.*

On no one you preside
Most regal of all,
Tallest of tall
Others are small.

With your mysterious eyes,
You are Mona Lisa of charm,
Cleopatra of power
And Sheba of wisdom.

The future holds you
High in the sky
A glittering star
Lighting the way.

To sons and daughters
Of familiar faces,
You are the witness
Of so many races.

To them you are the guide.
Guide them into
Concentrated time
That lies ahead.

And into the unknown
Of the known,
Which needs your protection
And affection.

*Behind each statue – a story,*
*But behind you, a tale*
*To tell*
*For generations to come.*

*You are a legend,*
*Cannot be forgotten,*
*A shining image*
*From an age long gone.*

*Did you hear the ships' sirens*
*Crossing the Atlantic?*
*Did you bid farewell*
*To the Titanic?*

*Lifeless statues with no feeling*
*They are no match for you.*
*All is created for no meaning,*
*But to serve the few.*

*To the millions*
*You are a desire,*
*Setting their hearts*
*On fire.*

Do you have a secret wish,
Does you glory vanish in mist?
Don't you need a chair
Or bed to relax?

A greeting from us all,
Standing slender and tall,
Inspiring the human race –
You smart girl with the beautiful face.

All cities are envious
Of your New York
Because of you,
Standing at Hudson fork.

Finally may I call you, Statue of Identity,
Standing alone as eternity,
Dividing liberty from vanity,
Tell me, what do you know of your city?

Good night and good morning
You city of hunger
That never sleeps
For ever and ever.

*Caring for all needs*
*For guests and residents*
*From the homeless and poor*
*To kings and presidents.*

*You are truly a city for all*
*Shades and colours-*
*Old and young,*
*Tall, small and others.*

*You are incomparable.*
*You are unique.*
*Your air radiates*
*Unmistakeable mystique.*

*Every minute is a start*
*For a business or romance*
*Racing forward not to miss*
*That last chance.*

*Every minute is a start,*
*For a play, a film or dance,*
*To be watched and be applauded,*
*On the street or on the stage.*

*Every minute is a start*
*For a smile or a glance,*
*At a friend or at a stranger,*
*To be tested sometime later.*

*Every minute is a start*
*For an actor to be a star,*
*For a painter to be famous,*
*For a singer to be known.*

*Every minute is a start*
*For a nation to be born*
*For a war to be fought*
*For the UN to be brought.*

*Every minute is a start*
*For some money to be gained*
*Or a fortune to be lost,*
*Wall Street is the place.*

*New York is a disco*
*Of elegant buildings*
*Dancing to the song*
*Of the Manhattan skyline.*

*Views of happenings along the streets*
*Convey the very simple truths,*
*Here it's easy to make it*
*And so very easy to fall.*

*Window on the world,*
*From the World Trade Centre,*
*At 106th Floor to see and be seen –*
*What a world to enter.*

*Further down the avenues*
*Broadway and 42nd Street,*
*Fame and famous at Times Square,*
*Doff their hats when they meet.*

*Riding horses and carriages*
*In Central Park,*
*Sparkling lights from stretching buildings,*
*Peeping in the dark.*

*Sightseeing*
*In Harlem streets*
*Where Jazz and Soul*
*Are played with ease.*

*The Plaza is the place to be*
*Alone, with friends or family,*
*Everyone is a walking story,*
*Ready for discovery.*

*A city of thousand and one nights*
*That dresses several dresses a night.*
*Your scent is art and culture,*
*Your make up is painting and sculpture.*

*Why do you love the company*
*Of museums and of galleries,*
*Movies and theatres,*
*Exhibitions and Convention Centres?*

*You are a city of many friends,*
*Who are hungry for your charm*
*And eager for a date*
*For the dreams of wonderland.*

*Farewell New York*
*The living nerve of imagination*
*The focus of creation*
*The city of many names.*

*But you are still a city of hunger*
*Which has created wonders*
*For the world to remember*
*A long time after.*

## *CITY OF DEFIANCE*

*I am Paris today*
*And Paris tomorrow*
*I am the pretty city –*
*And the rest to follow.*


*I am Paris to say,*
*And Paris to stay,*
*I am the pretty girl*
*With whom you play.*


*I am Paris I was*
*And Paris I rose;*
*The naughty child*
*With the red nose.*


*I was Paris the child*
*The child of whom?*
*Kings and Queens –*
*And I was the dream.*

*I am Paris the fun*
*And Paris the youth,*
*Keeping all guessing*
*But my friends know the truth.*

*I am Paris. I speak*
*All languages (including French).*
*In the language of romance*
*All I need is a bench.*

*I am Paris en vacances*
*For the tourists to see*
*All scenes are to be*
*A later memory.*

*I am Paris the old*
*And I am Paris the mode*
*My style is seductive*
*And my voice is attractive.*

I am Paris the chic
And Paris the name
My perfume's all over
And my fashion, the same.


I am Paris tonight
And Paris good night,
Take a romantic flight
In the city of light.


I am Paris the song
Where the poor belong
I am Paris the witch
The place for the rich.


I am Paris the durable
And I am Paris the adorable
Sometimes I am lonely,
And sometimes Les Miserables...

*I am Paris I live*
*And Paris I love*
*Five letters in name*
*Is all that I have.*


*I am Paris the culture*
*And Paris the art*
*My vision is to lead*
*From the early start.*


*I am Paris of politics*
*I taught the world the etiquette*
*The first lesson is*
*Not to remember and not to forget.*


*I am Paris of science*
*And Paris of firsts*
*In any fields you mention*
*I have passed the tests.*

*I am Paris the witness*
*For history to be made*
*The masses had marched*
*Demanding loaves of bread.*


*The Revolution had started*
*Regardless of Antoinette cake*
*The world had needed*
*An example to imitate.*


*I am Paris the memory*
*My past is anarchy*
*My present is harmony*
*My future will be –*


*Que sera sera*
*I will remain the defier*
*Flying higher and higher*
*Setting all hearts on fire.*

## *A CITY OF WISDOM*

*Beijing is a shrine
        of wisemen and wisdom.*

*Beijing is divine,
        an earthly kingdom.*

*The food, the wine,
        and the Chinese welcome.*

*A thought for the mind
        and spiritual freedom.*

*From Beijing you get the wisdom.*

*Beijing is a pearl,
        but who is the oyster?*

*Beijing is a pretty girl,
        but who is the father?*

*Beijing looks well,
        but who is the doctor?*

*Beijing rings the bell,
        but who is the conqueror?*

*Only wisemen have the answer.*

## *A CITY OF A NEW START*

*The name of Pretoria*
*Is all over the world.*
　　　　*Pretoria, Pretoria*

*The story of Pretoria*
*Is told and retold.*
　　　　*Pretoria, Pretoria*

*The trek to Pretoria*
*Is diamonds and gold.*
　　　　*Pretoria, Pretoria*

*The torch of Pretoria*
*Is in Mandela's hand.*
　　　　*Pretoria, Pretoria*

*The people of Pretoria*
*Are black and white*
*Living side by side.*
　　　　*Pretoria, Pretoria*

*The future of Pretoria*
*Is Africa's pride.*
　　　　*Pretoria, Pretoria*

*The glory of Pretoria*
*Is superior euphoria.*
　　　　*Pretoria the gloria*
　　　　*Pretoria the gloria*

# *ROME OF ROME*

*Rome of Rome*                     *Rome of Nero*
*Rome of Angelo*                   *Rome of heroes*
            *Rome of Rome*


*Rome of Romans*                   *Rome of fevers*
*Rome of Conquerors*               *Rome of Caesars*
            *Rome of Rome*


*Rome of Cities*                   *Rome of wonders*
*Rome of Paintings*                *Rome of sculptors*
            *Rome of Rome*


*Rome of the day*                  *And Rome of yesterday*
*Rome on the hills*                *And Rome of the wills*
            *Rome of Rome*


*Rome of Renaissance*              *Rome of learning*
*Rome of Arts*                     *And Rome of culture*
            *Rome of Rome*

Galileo for the science       Tower of Pisa of defiance
An eye in the sky               All stars to identify
                Rome of Rome

Leonardo and his inventions   Attracted world attention
Mona Lisa as a style          Enchanted us with her smile
                Rome of Rome

Rome of sighs               Rome of sights
Rome of centres          And Rome of theatres
                Rome of Rome

Rome of fountains         Rome of tombs
Rome of old                And Rome of new
                Rome of Rome

Rome of churches         Rome of domes
Rome of Popes             And Rome of hopes
                Rome of Rome

Rome of all                        Rome for all
Rome of the sun                Rome of fun
Rome of Rome

Rome of La Dolce Vita      Rome of Casanova
Rome of Ciccolina            Rome of Gigolos
Rome of Rome

Rome of inspiration         Rome of fascination
Rome of entrepreneurs     Rome of premieres
Rome of Rome

Rome of Verdi              Rome of operas
Rome of songs            And Rome of melodies
Rome of Rome

Rome of love               Rome in love
Rome of Arivederci       Rome of eternity
Goodbye to Rome

## *A DARLING CITY*

A darling city, married to the Nordic vanity,
With good fortune and destiny,
Destined to be a leading lady of sanity
It grew to be a daring city of immortality
Looking from above with wisdom and integrity.
                    Yes,
          Stockholm is a darling city.

A darling city that gave love to humanity,
Embraced every world activity,
Cared for every far away calamity,
And harmonized peace and tranquillity.
                    Yes,
          Stockholm is a darling city.

With her charm, elegance and grace.
Visitors in every place
Get impressed
With her blue and gold dress.
                    Yes,
          Stockholm is a darling city.

On her throne the witty, naughty
Lady city is sitting pretty.
                    Yes,
          Stockholm is a summer night city.
          Stockholm is a lovely city.

# SYDNEY THE HARBOUR

Sydney the harbour
    Attracted explorer after explorer.
Captain Cook and Sinbad the Sailor
    Had the honour to discover
That Sydney was for ever,
    And not on offer.
        Sydney is attraction.

It grew to be the other place
    For the human race.
With or without trace,
    With a new face
Sydney became an ace
    And a model case.
        Sydney is attraction.

Nurtured to be a melting pot
    For the whole lot,
From the haves and have nots
    To the cans and cannots.
It became the right spot
    For any type of sport.
        Sydney is attraction.

A sporty Sydney in every way,
    And come what may,
Riding the wave of the day,
    From bay to bay,
Cricket and rugby to play,
    On a sunny holiday.
        Sydney is attraction.

The dream of every maverick,
    To swim the Pacific,
To join the games of the Olympic,
    In this city of magic
When the fantasia is fantastic
    And Sydneysiders are terrific
        Sydney is attraction.

A stunning world to enter,
    A national park in every corner,
The Aborigines and their culture,
    Wild life all over,
The kangaroo and its neighbour,
    And a koala cuddling another.
        Sydney is attraction.

*Let us boomerang, you and me,*
*        Between the beaches and Coral Sea,*
*Rocks and reefs to eternity,*
*        Sing and dance in ecstasy,*
*Happy and carefree.*
*        Sydney is the place to be.*
*                Sydney is attraction.*

*The coat-hanger bridge*
*        And the opera house ridge*
*Are signs of a privilege*
*        Of a harmonious marriage*
*To the Sydney image,*
*        A city of colour and courage.*
*                Sydney is attraction.*

*From Perth to Darwin,*
*        Hand in hand with Melbourne,*
*Sydney and Canberra are the twins*
*        And the rest are next of kin,*
*But Sydney remains the foremost captain,*
*        From where many things begin.*

# A CORPORATE CITY

*Tokyo is a corporate city,*
*"Made in Japan" her identity,*
*Technology her equity,*
*And marketing her activity.*
*From Tokyo... to Tokyo...*


*From "war" to "peace"*
*Tokyo became a show piece,*
*Admired by world cities*
*As a pretty among the pretties*
*From Tokyo... to Tokyo...*


*From old to young*
*In Tokyo all sung*
*The Song of the Rising Sun*
*To the Emperor and his son*
*From Tokyo... to Tokyo...*

*From past to present*
*From ancient to recent*
*Traditions and customs*
*Face no problems*
*From Tokyo... to Tokyo...*


*From poor to rich*
*From millionaires to billionaires*
*The rule is unwritten*
*Hard work is a religion*
*From Tokyo... to Tokyo...*


*From cars to radios*
*And from electronics to videos*
*In Tokyo, everything is available*
*As long as it is profitable*
*From Tokyo... to Tokyo...*


*From Tokyo to Moscow*
*The Japanese will build a metro*
*A metro of trust and friendship*
*To all nations as a flag ship*
*From Tokyo... to Tokyo...*

*From Tokyo many things have come*
*Sumo wrestling on TV screen*
*Is now an enjoyable scene*
*Depicting the epic that had been*
*From Tokyo... to Tokyo...*


*From Tokyo you get a ritual*
*Among other rituals*
*Like tea drinking is an equal*
*Among other equals*
*From Tokyo... to Tokyo...*


*From Tokyo the corporate*
*A message to the earth planet*
*"We are part of mankind*
*And to your globe will be kind"*
*From Tokyo... to Tokyo...*


*To Tokyo on the hill of prosperity*
*Greeting from the world community*
*Hoping your example is a factor*
*For the world's peace and tranquillity*
*From Tokyo to tranquillity*

## *THE IDEAL CITY*

*This version is of a city*
*that has everything.*

*The Ideal City*
*Has a high tech entity*
*And futuristic identity.*

*The Ideal City*
*Has a computer in every house*
*And any required utility.*

*The Ideal City*
*Has the individuality*
*And the interactivity.*

*The Ideal City*
*Has the work force*
*Engaged in virtual reality.*

*The Ideal City*
*Has a touch of mystery*
*And human ingenuity.*

*The Ideal City*
*Has the availability*
*Of every opportunity.*

*The Ideal City*
*Has the ability*
*And the creativity.*

*The Ideal City*
*Has the fame, the name,*
*The money and credibility.*

*The Ideal City*
*Has the vitality*
*And happy community.*

*The Ideal City*
*Has the pleasure,*
*The leisure and prosperity.*


*This is an ideal city.*

*This version is of a city
that has nothing.*

*The Ideal City
Has no running water
And no electricity.*

*The Ideal City
Has no mayor
And no municipality.*

*The Ideal City
Has no police
And no criminality.*

*The Ideal City
Has no taxman
And no authority.*

*The Ideal City
Has no rich and poor,
But equality.*

*The Ideal City*
*Has no greed,*
*But hospitality.*

*The Ideal City*
*Has no cold, wind*
*Or humidity.*

*The Ideal City*
*Has no pollution*
*And dirty locality.*

*The Ideal City*
*Has no similarity:*
*It is simplicity.*

*In the Ideal City*
*All live in harmony*
*And tranquillity.*

*This is an ideal city.*

## PAINTINGS OF THE CITIES

Highlighting each city with a visual image to its poetic image is a way of adding one beauty to another. It is a way of dressing up a legend with a glittering dress; and what can be a better dress than a painting in the Deltaism style and fashion, tailored especially to its famous landmark?

The reader may be interested to know that those seventeen magnificent paintings preceding each poem are very special for two reasons:

The first reason is that those paintings, oil on canvas, are a new type of art which the author initiated some years ago. This type of art is mastered by a handful of artists.

The second reason is that the artist selected for this task of dress-making and crystallizing time and space of cities which we love and admire was Nathalie Beauvillain, a talented French artist who shines distinctly among those handful of Deltaists; and to Nathalie we must say 'thank you' for the paintings that gave beauty to these poems.

It is appropriate to include a few lines on the Deltaism concept so the reader can become familiarized with this type of art.

*What is Deltaism?*

- In brief, Deltaism could be described as post-Cubism, but its flexibility has surpassed Cubism. Its flexibility is achieved through its simplicity. As the name indicates, the Delta is the building block of Deltaism.
- The term Deltaism, itself coined by the author, derives from the mathematical method used by Newton for the calculation of infinitesimal figures.
- The Delta is also the fourth letter of the Greek alphabet, symbolized by the triangle, a geometrical figure which is not static, but free perpetually to become other, utterly and infinitely convertible. The core of the concept of Deltaism derives precisely from this potentiality, which is also posited as a new meeting point for art and science.
- Therefore Deltaism is, above all, seen as an interpretative instrument capable of changing the way with which we approach models, and, as such, it has to do with various forms of thought – from art to politics.
- In the final act, Deltaism has also its own philosophy of synergizing *Threesomeness* in conceiving excellence!

# SOUNDS OF THE POEMS

After you have gone through each poem, you may feel like reading them aloud yourself to gain additional enjoyment; or perhaps you would like to hear someone else doing the job. If so, please use the CD inserted inside the back cover just for that reason.

Listening to the poems of your favourite cities will give you additional excitement. Extra care has been taken to produce this recording. The author and his son read the poems and Antti Ikonen composed special music for each city to be blended with its poem.

As a closing remark, let us hope that this avantgarde way of city presentation, using poem, painting and sound, has been satisfying.